# Poetical Musings

## ON PIANOS, MUSIC & LIFE

### Volume II

♪♫♪

## Ann Grogan

# Readers' Comments

"Ann Grogan is truly a force to be reckoned with when she sets her mind to it. I have witnessed this in her many endeavors. First is her focused pursuit of creative expression through the piano, for many hours and years. Second is the refinement of her search ultimately culminating in the rebuilding of a nearly lost instrument. When the piano of her dreams was not found, she brought one back into the world by re-envisioning a lovely instrument on which she could stretch her wings, put in the hard work needed, and share her talents. As if that wasn't enough of an adventure, third, she explored another creative realm, poetry in words that document, detail, elucidate, and express her deep love for and humor regarding the piano. Not to mention that these poems tell the fortuitous story of her journey, which is wonderful to witness."

> — jordan hines, artist
> http://www.JordanHines.com

"I absolutely loved this second volume of light hearted poetry about playing the piano in maturity. "Andante" or "Allegro" particularly resonated as I try to live my life at an Andante tempo, while my brain tries to force Allegro upon me! And Grogan captures the state of flow at the piano with her poem "I Heard My Piano Play":

> "I heard her join in with what I played,
> but speak in a different voice,
> fuller and richer than I'd heard to date.
> I completed the phrase, but in a haze,
> wondering what I had heard?"

This is a great collection for older adults who brave the bench, and know what it is to love the piano, the process, the pain, and the deepest pleasure."

> — Gaili Schoen, author, *Upper Hands Piano: A Method for Adults 50 to Spark the Mind, Heart and Soul;*
> UpperHandsPiano.com

# Dedication

To anyone who has a song in their heart to sing,
and to those who have heard mine.

# Acknowledgments

With heartfelt thanks to Joe Torres, OD and to
Tung Vu for reading and commenting upon my
manuscript and, of course, for the continuing love,
patience, and technical support from my life partner,
Ron Choy (however, any remaining errors and
omissions are my responsibility).

# Introduction

Music has become a source of calm, peace, and wonder for me during the past three years. It started shortly after I retired at the beginning of 2020 from a 30-year career in the fashion business and a legal career that lasted 16 years before that. Early in the same year after the arrival of the pandemic, I felt an urgent need for solace, diversion, and to artistically express my deepest feelings about life and love; painting portraits of people or kitties just wasn't doing it. I decided to take piano lessons after not playing my high school spinet for 63 years! A year later the idea struck me to try out a grand piano just once in my life, and then return to playing my spinet.

A neighbor answered my online notice asking to "borrow" a grand piano to play in exchange for a home-cooked gourmet meal. I never expected the blessings that came when Joe Torres responded within the hour! His piano is a gorgeous seven-foot Beethoven Special Edition Bösendorfer. I immediately fell in love with its curvaceous, shiny black cabinet and its silky tones and famed bass sounds. Now I had an inkling of how a grand piano differed in tone and touch from my spinet. It was only a few days later when I decided that I just had to have a grand piano, too!

To find the perfect small grand that would fit into one corner of our modest-sized living room wasn't as easy as I thought, or as inexpensive. In fact, my projected budget doubled over the ten months of my search. Finally, Bruce Nalezny, a Bay Area pianist, composer, and piano broker, found a dusty, disheveled, original 1928 Steinway Model M covered up in the corner of a workshop attached to a piano retail store. Bruce assured me that it had a pristine soundboard and an amazingly sustained tone when it was played, especially in the often-weak fifth and sixth octaves.

The soundboard is a critical feature that sometimes can be repaired, but is terribly expensive to replace, so I decided to take a leap of faith and have this piano rebuilt. It seemed much better than continuing an arduous process of playing piano-after-piano, when nothing for sale in piano stores or private homes seemed just right.

The six-month wait for the piano was excruciating. She was finally complete and moved in on April 28, 2022. Over the weeks I found myself drawn to practice more and more hours each day, and I fell more deeply in love with music. I named her *Rhapsody-Arabesque, DMB* (*The Duchess of Music and Bliss*). Before starting my warm-up exercises, I usually sit and admire the beauty of her silky, reddish-gold hand-rubbed cabinet that I had refinished to match our teak furniture (Jeff Harris, a neighbor friend, gave her the clever nickname of *Miss Teak*). I can hardly resist lightly brushing my fingers over the unique platinum-colored metal Steinway & Sons logo placed just above the pristine ivory keys. Then I start to work so that I can more artistically express the deep love I have for music and my piano.

I initiated a breakfast "music appreciation hour" by preparing an omelette, sitting down to eat, and reading a chapter or two in a musicology book or pianist's biography. I also listen to a known or newly discovered composition and am often inspired to write a poem. I keep a growing list of these compositions which amount to over 500 by today. This was, and remains, a deeply satisfying way to begin my day because it fires my brain, body, and spirit. Then I am motivated to do my morning exercises and sit down at *The Duchess* to undertake the first part of my daily practice regime.

What could be a better way to spend happy, productive hours during retirement?  I hope you, too, enjoy many of the same kinds of hours, and are inspired by music!

— Ann Grogan  ♪♫♪

# Table of Contents

# On Poetry

♪♫♪

"Poetry is a political act,
because it involves telling the truth."

— June Jordan,
Jamaican American poet

Fig.1  The original *Duchess,* a dark, disheveled 1928
       Steinway Model M on the day Ann first played her,
       October 16, 2021.

On Poetry

Poetry is therapy, poetry gives hope.
What? You want me to sit at home and mope
when I can pour my heart into a receiving cup
then read back my words and know I'm heard
by someone important to my soul–
just me, and then I more easily come to understand
what this or that experience meant,
what lesson I was to learn and then carry on,
moving along my path, my decisions made,
some hopes finely wrought but not to be,
other hopes from blue skies come home to me
about how to be, or move, or think,
or live, or love, or what poem to ink.

# Themes

Is there a theme in what I write?
One of joy or one of plight,
one of angels, one of sin,
in the poems that I pen
when in the mood I do pursue
a thought, along with my trusty muse?

There certainly is, I see it well–
and more than one that I can tell!
The first is fun, the same with bliss,
then next The One, and then a kiss
and touch, then letting go, letting abide
the soul that lives so deep inside.

I use "repose" a lot I see,
when writing all my poetry.
I must feel tired, I'm sure I do
when facing down my demons true
and seeing how short life really is,
making moments precious in what they give.

# This I Can Say

Steven Isserlis, the noted cellist
and author of two children's books, too,
organizer of a famed musical conference,
recapitulates piano advice by Schu.*

Impressive both authors, no less two musicians,
Isserlis, a giant with "leading orchestras" it seems,
so says the book jacket of the pretty gift book
that Isserlis wrote, published first in '16.

I mused about Isserlis as an "outstanding performer,"
whose "quirky and humorous writing"
pleased musical magazines; he elicited much praise
by including his own advice, also inspiring.

But in this, my modest musical poetry book,
no famed conference plaudits can I sing,
no outstanding performances can I list,
but a few lovely comments on my book jacket ring.

But this I do promise in these few words,
this I can assure you right from the start,
my experience is real, both joyful and sad,
and my poems come to you from my truest heart.

———
*"Schu" is my favorite, easily-rhyming, perhaps irreverent,
nickname for Robert Schumann, famed Romantic period
composer, author, and music critic. In 2016 Isserlis wrote
a lovely, small gift book entitled *Robert Schumann's Advice
to Young Musicians, Revisited by Steven Isserlis*, and
included some of his own cogent advice.

# No Words

She never had *no* words to say,
of that I'm very sure.
Sometimes she cursed or even worse—
for talking there was no cure.

So, imagine this (I'm sure you can't):
a lawyer stands up in court
but hasn't a clue about what to say?
An impossibility of sorts!

Or imagine a mother whose recent joy
is caused by the babe in hand:
she doesn't croon the softest tune
and tell him he's the best in the land?

Now imagine a piano without a song:
she silently sits there,
a piece of furniture in that dead case
at which all just sit and stare?

There's only one state, a state of grace,
where no words will flow at all:
when a lover beholds his beloved near
and to love, Mr. Cupid calls.

*Seven Poems*

Seven in one day?
This is a true obsession,
at least that's my impression.
No matter what, sane or insane,
neurotic or nonsense,
it's what I feel and think and want
and the way that I am bent!


*On Criticism of Poetry*

Anodyne I'll never be;
a bee lives under my bonnet.
I'll often tell you, like it or not,
what I think of your plain sonnet
as I wax poetic, sometimes ekphrastic,
about elements of music
and say just what I think
if you give me prideful rubric.

But that's only if you ask my opinion,
otherwise I'll remain dead quiet.
It's *your* life, *your* poetry,
and what *you* want
to represent your life.

# *Passion and The Poet*

Passion a poet does not make
(one critic told me that),
nor intelligent use of words or rhyme;
or things I overlooked–oh, drat!

I failed "to apply poetry protocols"
from a "magnificent" tradition quite ancient,
so nothing of value she found to discuss,
save "good vocabulary" and "evident passion."

How nice–I'll take them! She got my main message,
to love life and jump in to express
the things that bring you joy and hope,
brain power and all the rest!

Go take up an instrument, attend the symphony,
discuss music with your friends,
suffer a beginner's status as a "pianist"
with the challenges that it brings.

And as for poetry, I'll consider critiques,
remembering in the main
what one favored writer, Mencken, said
in words so perfectly plain:

**"It is astonishing how voluptuously
criticism cherishes nonsense."**
*H.L. Mencken on Music.*

# Who Knew?

I write ekphrastic poetry
(an editor told me that).
Sounds pretty erudite—
makes me sound like one cool cat.

I guess the 'phrastic part
deals with the musical arts,
such as how one composes
and how the chills do start.

The goal of ekphrasis
is to make the subject visual,
but in the case of invisible music
the process becomes more magical.

I imagine that I could write
a hyperbolic disquisition
on the physics of the overtone
or how a sonata's begun.

But I prefer the simple,
not besot with embellishing,
though truth be told and I so bold,
I'd declare my love for Chopin!

# On How Poetry Comes

Sometimes I'll take a spin
flying low,
missing buildings as I go;
the words come out
in a haphazard way
and I fly circles around them.

Sometimes dizzy, tumbling thoughts
not well thought out
or fraught with deepest feelings
take control,
then rudderless I helpless fall
in love, or trouble in my flight.

Sometimes I miss my mark,
or on a lark take higher flight,
remember some pang or failed attempt
to reach a goal, some jailed desire
that had me on fire
wanting more.

Sometimes I soar,
the meaning clear
as words roar in my ear
about love lost, but more gained,
and I pen my pain or bliss
because I missed not one thing in life!

# On Music & Musicology

♪♫♪

"Music, being identical with heaven, isn't a thing of
momentary thrills, or even hourly ones.
It's a condition of eternity."

– Gustav Holst,
English composer,
arranger, and teacher

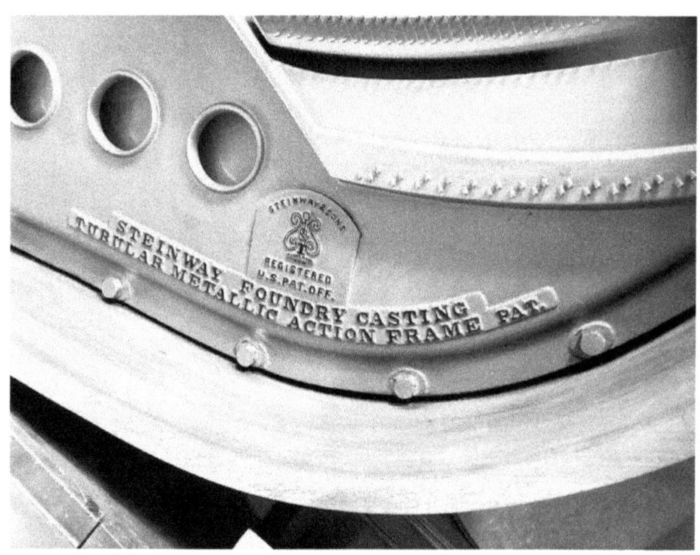


Fig. 2   Interior of *The Duchess'* 1928 iron plate and
Steinway name.

# Music Is Love

Are music and love the same?
Both dissolve social hierarchy.*
Both contain the seeds of redemption.
Both negate the patriarchy.

More than a source of pleasure, the two,
the embodiment of pleasure per se!
Both seek to defeat shame as we claim
our right to a happy day.

To feelings of "less than" we readily fall victim,
to labels we cling as lifeline,
but both of those things will strangle us with
thoughts of the negative kind.

Societies, our families, and sometimes the church
that often lurch about unbound,
cast not love but hate upon our souls,
leaving no niche where hope can be found.

Truth rings out in music and in love,
and once more it's easy to see
that you and I are the same beneath bonds
that wrap us and keep us unfree.

So boldly, go declare this just cannot be!
We won't deny pleasure or hope,
we won't fight a war or never care for others,
for with music and love, we will cope!

---

*These three cogent ideas about love come from Dr. Carol
Gilligan's book, *The Birth of Pleasure.* The idea that music
does the same because it *is* the same as love, is my own.

## Tipsy

Could she be the Juliet of Romeo's daydreams
basking in the warmth of lazy Sunday's sunbeams?
Sweet melodies bring contentment;
she, adrift in repose,
grateful for the gift from her friend's creative cosmos.*

---

*Inspired upon receiving an unexpected and appreciated birthday
gift of *Ten Pieces for Children* by composer Bruce Nalezny
(bruce@finepiano.com); Tipsy is one of my three kitties.

# My Job After Retirement

This is my job, to play piano,
that is my love for sure!
There's nothing nicer in my world
than music, I can assure,
unless to enhance my harmonious dream
with the company I procure,
I share my love though I truly am
a pianistic amateur.

At day's news of war and famine
it's easy to turn dour
and a blue and dismal mood prevails
if I don't pursue this cure
and play my pieces, oft sing along
to banish what I abjure
and allow the music to lift me up.
Though I could be a bit unsure,
thus, come the calm and peace within—
in that, I remain secure.

# Something About Music

There's something about music
that's grabbed my soul,
turned me inside out
and my spirit roiled.
More than dance that sets me free
or when painting rocks my world,
music came to abide with me
to help my soul unfurl.
"Open to the wind" is what Webster's says
is the definition of "unfurl."
And so it does, this magical gift:
the music I now hear, and heard.

*For Those Who Listen*

Form and emotion, A. Storr* says,
propel the argument
that one or the other does prevail.
It's no accident
that to appreciate someone's composition
takes more than narrow views
of just the form. The listener
adds an element, too,
and so confounds the bloody matter!

If new music, then form
prevails to focus attention
while emotions pale so often.
But give us memory of a piece well known,
and emotions may hold sway;
we sense the structure embedded there,
our pleasure not delayed.

Form and content, body and soul,
in humans indivisible;
if one comes first or last, at last,
no matter to the sensible!

---

*Anthony Storr (1920-2001), *Music and the Mind.* This book
is my favorite book about music and musicology. Dr. Storr
was a respected British psychiatrist, author, journalist, and
radio and TV commentator who had a keen love of music
and literature as well as medicine and psychiatry. He played
the viola and sang in the choir of Winchester College.

# Inner Voices 1: Some Questions

In these questions lies a poem
about a musical topic mysterious:
it's called "inner voices," of that I'm sure,
a phrase I find so curious.

To start my research, some questions I outlined
to flesh out the answers that hide:
are they notated only in the treble,
if there the main melody resides?

Or are they merely separate melodies
that occur in treble and bass,
like Mozart liked to use most times
as his music us did grace?

And do these voices, if they exist,
ever transform at all
to main melodies, or melody, if one,
or disappear from the chorale?

And how the heck do I identify
an inner voice to look up,
and concerning such notes–if they exist,
do the stems go down or up?

So quest I now for answers certain,
my research cut out for me;
I'll start with friends, then the internet,
and won't forget Siri!

# *Inner Voices 2: More Focused Questions*

Is a counter melody the same thing
as a true inner voice?
And is this phrase only applicable to
chorales for four equal voices?

Is harmony required, no less a pitch
one can easily identify,
to have a hope of every finding
where an inner voice does lie?

So lying 'twixt bass and soprano
is where inner voices I'll find?
And is dissonance more acceptable
inside the main melody line?

Are outer voices the highest voice
and bass the lowest one,
with the inner voice softer by far
than the other singing tone?

Are there particular styles of music,
that tend to have such voices
making them easier to hear and identify
among all the myriad choices?

Is there a "leading tone" in an inner voice
and need it be resolved?
Some say not so, and with them I'll go
(is my puzzle now being solved?).

––––––––––

*For an excellent video explaining and demonstrating how
inner voices sound versus the melody line, see a video on
classical pianist Robert Estrin's website: https://livingpianos.
com/3-piano-technique-tips-lessons-from-robert-estrin/

As we move along our musical way,
keep room for more to come.
There's no end to rewards that us await
and the journey's never done.

Just when we think a piece is learned
and we've reached our single goal,
what we've accomplished can be much more
than just a single mile pole.

There's reward enough to one's soul
to reach the end of effort
and cement the progress in one's memory
and then just remain alert.

But then there comes another thought,
the recognition there's more
to playing the piano and making music
than judging by just one score.

There's the friend who listens in
and we brighten up her day,
or a frustrated mom who scoops a child up,
sits down, and a duet plays,

And those who weep may find solace
with sad songs in a minor key,
or celebrate a success in sport,
with a parade as destiny.

For romance, the music of Barry White,
for calm, the plaintive violin,
express conflict with twelve-tone technique
or crashing chords of Beethoven.

Music is the universal language
that needs no words or spin.
You'll always find the perfect piece
to suit what mood you're in!

## Who's On Top?

Can one love be more serious than any other?
Does one parent love one daughter over the other?
Can we choose who lives or dies
between two equal brothers?
Is one composer really greater than another?
Could single never exceed the joys of being a mother?
Why is "who's on top?"
more important than the bother
to simply appreciate just what you'd druther?


## Andante or Lento?

I like *andante.*
I relate.
Life at my stage
moves with all deliberate speed
as appropriate to my age.
All so good! I would continue,
noting how fast the days of *allegro* go
(not to mention *vivacissimo*),
my first movement, now past.
Nothing lasts. The lesson of tempo
just about learned, more than an inkling
staring me in the face
(for any pace from *grave* to *presto*),
what matters now
is what I always said
when embarking on dreams that I had:

If *lento*...at least I'm "Go!"

## May I Smile?

Is music so serious
that I can't be deliriously happy when I play
or listen to the music that rings
from YouTube and like things?
Will someone insist I keep my face
in a serious place
and make it stay that way?

But how can I, when there exist
such lovely souls so bold,
like Danny Kaye
holding sway over
the Philharmonic?*
That sweet maniac leaves the stage
to allow his orchestra to meet the test
of playing best, or just as well
as anyone could tell with Kaye on stage!

What about Palmer,** a quite devilish tease
who makes poor Tchaikovsky turn in his grave
with her cute antics playing his concerto at hand?
She makes me laugh with intentional gaffs
and breaks us all up in smiles.

Then there's Peter the Schickele***
of South North Dakota fame,
The "Professor of Musical Pathology,"
yet from Julliard he came!

---

*"An Evening with Danny Kaye" and the New York
Philharmonic; https://www.youtube.com/watch?v=
zIHS6S8NVRQ
**Amanda Palmer is an American singer, songwriter,
musician, and performance artist; see her hilarious
"Cell Phone Interruption;" https://www.youtube.
com/watch?v=iBxF9UvDp/dU
***Peter Schickele is a composer-musician known for
his musical satire; https://en.wikipedia.org/wiki/P._D._Bach

So clever this devil
who beguiles as he conducts
an orchestra of instruments
including whistles, pans, and pots,
duck calls and all
loosed upon the land.
We smile as his special music rings
in honor of his patron saint,
"P.D.Q. Bach," the 21st son (he claims)
of 20 that there were
(of that we are aware),
or at least he said
with a perfectly straight face,
putting elitists squarely in their place!


## So Many Angels


We've missed so many angels, haven't we?
They choose to play today in another place
so far away from us.
I lament with the elegy that sounds in my mind
for those who left before I awoke,
the solace that I missed, the miracle of music
they offered to share when times coincided,
the student ready to learn or the listener to hear
what they offered us,
our musical Greats, so revered,
but now passed on.

# More Love

No man of war can love music,
no enslaved woman, too,
though names be writ upon a score
pretending that they do.

No man of hate who loves the game,
and the patriarchal paradigm,
can make music though he claims it true
when he just wastes our time,
as does the woman who lost her mind
and puts asunder the truth she knows,
falling silent in impure desire
for perceived riches vile men bestow.

No warring men can justify
hateful acts that know no bounds,
reenacting what their fathers did
in the old one-up/one-down.
No decent man believes in his heart,
that some do not belong
to the human race, no less the case
for women who know that's wrong.

Though warring demons of vilest nature
can cause us mortal wounds,
they also leave music in disarray
and kill the pure pleasure of love.
For to love music requires that we love,
even making mistakes we regret,
and then we remember what we know,
that love more love begets.

*Inspired by the request of B.N. to write a poem about
the reasons that violence continues against powerless
people via war and in personal relationships.

# Answering

I wonder why I buy more scores
I certainly can't immediately play,
then each one goes into my store
of pieces I'll take up someday?
I thought about that puzzling question
and here's just what I'll say:
each score upon arrival surely
brightens up my day!

Not only that, I'm sure you know,
each represents the hope
that someday soon my love can show
for what the composer wrote,
no less the appreciation that I feel
for music light or austere
that inspires me to express myself
and lift up those who hear.

For once I know and fall in love–
it happens in just an instant–
and feel the chills come down my spine,
then to resist, I really can't.
Any melody that to me speaks out
and leads me to my home
lets me know I've naught to fear
and will never be alone.

## The First

Is the first the best?
The very first version of what we play–
or our first kiss?
Does refinement tend to grow with practice
and with age?
Does it depend on the stage of life
or the day we try to express our very best?

But if the worst?
Must we stand still and stare and wonder
where's the thrill
and what should come next, we ponder?
Could be the second will be better
if we heave a sigh and try another then another?
Why bother? Because we can–no lie!

Start first to listen deep within,
search for the sound and then
the sweet and light and pure delight, then try again.
You'll win this time, don't brook one doubt!
Just move and play
first from within and then out.
Think the notes, think the sound,
a tone hard or round?
Imagine that you travel far beyond a star
and enter into the welcoming black hole of oblivion
and become One,
where all melodies and harmonies begin.

# Food for Thought

I'd like to be arpeggiated,
perhaps even massiagiated,
definitely satiated and
maybe even marinated?

I'd like some rubato,
on my hamburger, a tomato,
possibly a baked potato
and certainly a legato.

Study me an etude,
dance me a pavanne,
circle me a rondo,
then feed me a flan.

Nothing's better than music
to feed the soul
or when eating whipped cream
as a concerto unfolds.

# On Composers, Compositions & Musicians

♪♫♪

"Music is a moral law. It gives soul to the universe,
wings to the mind, flight to the imagination, and charm
and gaiety to life and to everything."

– Plato

Fig. 4   *The Duchess'* logo and original ivory keys.

# Fritz

This is the melody that completely enthralls
beyond others that to my heart do call,
the Sorrow Song* soft by Fritz Kreisler
that on my ears does sweetly fall.
The reason for him, a remarkable violinist,
the best I've heard, I do believe
(though music critic I may not be),
beyond argument, I plainly can see:
this man is an angel guided from above,
luckily brought to earth down below,
destined to give to us mere mortals
his touch of gold and make us glow.

---

*"Leibesleid" by violinist Fritz Kreisler (1875-1962), an
Austrian-born American violinist and composer; one of
the most noted violin masters of his day and one of my
two favorite violinists (the other is Ivry Gitlis).

# No Way

I want to poetize Lupu, but I can't.
Would be beyond cant and worse to try.
The very most I can do is sigh
and go on my way,
allowing music to have its way
and listen to Radu play
the Brahms Piano Concerto No. 1
in D minor,* Saraste conducting.
There's nothing left to say.

---

*From a 1996 concert. Pianist Radu Lupu (1945-2022) was a
Romanian pianist widely recognized as one of the greatest of
his time, having an ineffable touch and exquisite sound;
https://www.youtube.com/watch?v=79lbldvXzFc

# *Streaming*

I was outside in my garden on a summer day
when San Francisco fog comes and goes
(mostly comes late in the day),
with a gentle breeze as I stood midst wafting scents
of roses, jasmine, and four lavender plants,
gently swaying in time to…music that I heard!

Coming through my open window
where the song had moved on
from what I had listened to several times that day
(Borodin's Notturno No. 2 for String Quartet
as transcribed for piano by V. Gryaznov),*
music now new to my senses:
M. Ravel's "Daphnis et Chloé Suite No. 2"
for not one, but pianos two!

The notes wrapped me 'round and did embrace
and kiss my face and gently take my hand
as I stood transfixed in an unbelievable land
of streaming notes and rumbling ocean waves
of deepest sound that greeted me.
As I stood, my magic carpet lifted off the sand
into blue skies with puffy clouds
that did surround me then.
I disappeared in and out, with spiraling turns
and twists of pure delight in my flight.

I cannot say how long I spent flying that day,
standing there, allowing this music to urge me on
and eventually takes its place upon
the wisps of endless time in my mind.

---

*The score transcribed for two pianos from Ravel's concerto, by
one of my favorite pianists, Vyacheslav Gryaznov, a Russian
classical pianist, recording artist, transcriber, composer, and
assistant professor of piano; https://www.youtube.com/watch?v=
VeHCFsjQr8o

# Benediction

Listen to Ciccolini* tickle lightly
each protrusion of your spine
and send chills up that lovely
undulating wave to the stars above
and connect our bodies to the heavens
as Liszt he plays, a benediction on us all
before we fall away, as we must,
in trust that the clouds will meet us there
and lift us up to sit in silent awe
and listen to this Maestro play.

---

*Aldo Ciccolini (1925-2015), Italian pianist, teacher, and
celebrated interpreter of French composers, with over 100
recordings and a 50-year career (Satie was among his students).
Consider "Benediction of God in Solitude" by Liszt, especially
the second movement; https://www.youtube.com/watch?
v=231R1VOX_3o


# A Challenge

How wrong some pundits are to say
that thrills come from surprise;
there's no surprise in "Confidence,"*
yet repeated chills arise.
I dare you to take up the score
and hear the melodious tones
that gift this piece with a magical call
to mount upon the throne,
then see what thrills you experience
as sweet notes come your way,
and chills ripple up and down your spine
to hear the piece you play.

---

*The sweet piece by Mendelssohn is from a collection
of 48 songs for solo piano, *Lied Ohne Worte*.

# Totentanz

The poor piano will give up,
lay down its arms, after a pianist
wreaks harm on its keys.
The Bataan Death March has nothing on this piece!
Obviously overwrought, Liszt sought
to overwhelm us with variations
on "Dies Irae," so they say.

Call her "Liszt-ica" one person says of Lisitsa,
Russian virtuosa of pianistic fame
who engenders "Brava!"
as her hands flow like lava over keys
in "Totentanz," a dance of death.

But I prefer Pace, whose hands disappear
below the keys in roaring opening chords
of this insane piece.
His ability need I defend?
Can you resist his call to attend?
Emilio compels on his journey through hell
as the music ebbs and swells.
So listen at leisure, but plan not to sleep;
there's no rest in store when Pace's company you keep!

# "Salon" vs. "Serious"; Really?

Why is some music more "serious" than another?
Why would some deem lighter music "salon,"
and then not bother?
So what is "salon" music and why take pains to diss it?
Why would one not want to receive all
and not just have a fit?
Must be some man in commenting on Chaminade,*
who deigns he has the answer to a woman's aspiration
when he had no idea at all.
Again we hear the paternalist eternalist
into "one-up/one-down,"
a thought that to my cheery face
always brings a frown.
Music is no competition: sir, take heed!
Or from an imagined dagger, you may one day bleed!

------

Writer "Gamma 1734" says in comments to Cecile Chaminade's
Piano Sonata in C minor on YouTube: "Very influenced by
Schumann the brillant (sic) main theme lacks a very convincing
development-I have the feeling as she was seen as Salon
composer she wanted to compose something 'serious'. The last
movement for example is of similar style to her Toccata. Chopin's
Piano Sonata 1, 5th Movement, is more convincing in comparison.
All in all beautiful composition;" https://www.youtube.com/
watch?v=L4IjloAwgd4

*Liszt-This*

There is Liszt-this, Schumann-that,
and Chopin in the main,
I love Mendelssohn more, and do you implore
to understand most modernists I disdain.

Tchaikovsky lives within my hands,
and easy reach is he
into my heart with his ballet art
since I wanted a dancer to be.

In search of missing parts in the musical arts
I found C. Chaminade,
her Etude* exudes the sweetest sound,
with Amy Beach not far behind!

But when I listen to Christa Ludwig
at her concluding concert in Vienna,**
time dissolves and so do I,
leaving me the sweetest dilemma:

Which song is best? Just one of many
she sings as her final adieu,
and that is "Morgen" by Richard Strauss–
and I am born anew.

---

*"Autumn" Etude Opus 35 No. 1 by C. Chaminade;
https://www.youtube.com/watch?v=AuGuwRYa0GE
**"Tribute to Vienna Concert" 1994, final recital by Christa
Ludwig; https://www.youtube.com/watch?v=CTK6ffHQucs

And now, for a little bawdy humor which helps us
rebalance and calm our spirits after hearing the daily
news, then recenter ourselves in the magic of music.


## Hauser


I'm enthralled by Hauser, the maestro,
the most gorgeous, long-haired fellow;
unparalleled odd facial antics,
while stroking his bow so frantic,
but I'm more captivated by the size of his cello.


## Gryaznov


Slava is certainly not grava!
He makes me start flowing like lava,
he's a sight for sore eyes,
the best virtuoso prize–
if a woman, I'd call out "Brava!"


## Yuja Wang


As cute as a bug in a rug
quite deserving of the warmest hug!
A powerhouse of talent
her reputation does cement,
all else is merely humbug!


## Buniatishoili (courtesy of author J.B.)


Khatia sits so beautifully nude,
privately completing her etude–
a fantasy so dreamy
and alluringly steamy,
it's a rapturous morning interlude!

Fig. 5   On a happy lesson day!

# On Music Theory, Piano Lessons & Practice

♪♫♪

"The notes I handle no better than many pianists.
But the pauses between the notes—
ah, that is where art resides!"

– Artur Schnable
*Chicago Daily News,*
June 11, 1958

Fig. 5    Ann with her neighbor pianist friend, Joe Torres, OD,
          whose generosity in allowing her to play his gorgeous
          Bösendorfer grand piano, sparked her idea to own her
          own grand piano!

# An Amateur Pianist's Prayer

May I be just who I am
and not compare how I would be
and how I hear and what I hold dear,
had I but begun at age two or three?

May I hold on, do what I'm able,
never fall into despair
or write my epitaph before the flow
when I can express just what I hear?

May I have time to learn to play
the simplest song and melody,
not letting ego lead me on
to bigger dreams that divert me?

May I expect a welcome touch,
from those who know just what I hear
and lead me forward with the kindest grace
to join the ecstasy in music's place?

May I have grace to go inside
while music plays itself through me,
and as I sit at my *Duchess* fair,
unity in music and life come clear?

# To Be A Late Senior Piano Student*

and someday soon, I'll play!
oh, but glorious, sunny day–
I think I'll try again;

Keep faith, there's effort needed to succeed!
All must bleed, concert genius, too–and you.

cry.
and often
and learn to walk again,
baby stage you must return to
defeat you: imagined shame as to the
Even if the time is free, it fleets. Do not let
balance of the body, ego, and no less, the soul.
kept in mind; how to get there by self or others;
More than clever needed: clear definition of end goals
begin a long trek but not among the stars, not close yet.
Takes a lot to learn piano! I must ascend a high hill and

———————
*It will make sense to read this poem from the bottom line up
while imagining that you are climbing a high hill.

# Lost Cause

Am I a lost cause because
I'm not from a musical family?
Liszt, a child, taught by his father,
Clara Schumann, too,
so is it pedigree that's required to excel?
But at what? Doesn't that depend
on what my end is, my goal,
and what shores I flounder on
and whether waves take me out
or I fight a bout, never giving up,
taking just one wave,
at least one at a time,
time not being with me.

And yet it is,
in seconds here, then past,
just as fast as your seconds go, or hers,
that sweet marvel of the many curls,
or the long-hair pianistic Romeo.
So can I last the time it takes to
learn my fate at the piano,
or will I give up too soon?
I doubt that!
Not my nature to lose a fight,
not the way I've lived my life,
so why start now? Just plow ahead,
hell bent on getting there,
not to the stage but to *The Duchess* fair,
in her bowery where await
The Greats to take me by the hand
and guide me through their musical land.

## Higher Level?

Am I a "higher level" musician?*
What a troubling proposition
as to what that title bestows?
The "bestest" I suppose?
Then when will that happen
and the throne I may ascend?
A clear patriarchal notion
of "one-up/one-down" position,
giving egos a lift of import
to folks of that sorty-sort,
usually men (it's sad to note)
who enjoy that kind of stroke.

————

*Impelled (not inspired) upon hearing the phrase
used by a male violin teacher and professional
violinist in a major US orchestra.


## Typewriter Pianism

I shouldn't like to "play like a typewriter"
as dear Horowitz proclaimed,
about how some pianists pluck the strings
in a style he so disdained.
He meant the attack of a pianist's touch
that transmitted not one whiff
of spirit, but elicited recoil
and Horowitz's gentle fit.
I'm pretty sure that's not my sin,
nor hunt and peck my style.
I've feeling galore but need much more
to practice tempo with The General,*
then learn to bring a finer touch
to make my melody sing,
and tampen down the bass-most parts
to delicate nuances bring.

————

*Nickname I gave my metronome shortly after sighing,
then eventually agreeing to use it regularly in practice.

# Let Go

One cannot force piano love
because it may turn to hate,
no more than one can force a cloud
to change where it navigates.

One cannot make the sun to shine
or the rain to stop its patter,
though some may believe a magic wand
is the trick that will really matter.

I'd be a fool to ask for love
if you've nothing left to give,
just because it feels down deep
that without you I cannot live.

Since melody resides in willing hearts
that open to the music,
let go, accept, and remember hope-
those love bring, if you believe it.

## Like Life

Playing the piano is like life,
full of fun and sometimes strife,
or sometimes chills and then a kiss.
Perhaps a frown will take you down,
next day you're up to take a run
and enjoy the rays of morning's sun.
So life goes on its merrie way
with little choice in how we play
our instrument or role
or what we hear in our soul.


## How?

How can we fly if we cannot visit dread?
How can we live if we think only of the dead?
How can we sail if we're petrified of water
and don't notice how buoyed up
are friends like the otter?
How do we dance, if we don't take that first step?
How do we express love without eyes and our lips?
How do we protest without seizing the moment
and speak out in resistance to an obvious torment?
How do we thrive in a creative world
unless we speak truth unvarnished and unfurled?
How can we touch another human being
without allowing ourselves sometimes to be seen?


## Our Piano Duet

I'll be ready and oh, so steady
when we play our duet, we two
I promise you I'll practice lots,
not in set slogs giving short shrift
to what will lift spirits high
as we comply with composers' wills,
our listeners to thrill!

# The Lark

Just before the memory comes,
when the mission seems so dire,
all seems to defeat my every push
to realize a strong desire
to put aside the arranger's notes,
my comfort and my repose,
until the melody locks in
to brain, body, and soul.

Just before the plane can land
and the pilot breathes at last,
the one who plays must give way
to patience in the task
and play on in hopes that the endeavor
will surely come to calm,
when one day the lark awakes
and sings her heartfelt song.

# Retrograde

Loving corsets and hats and such,
the lady went on her way
with painted lips and pearls and rings
to brighten up her day.
Colors galore encircled her,
and spring came out to play,
her day's dress was more or less
a rainbow on display.
Scarves wound her body with silken touch,
as she happily skipped on,
living a life starkly out of touch
with all prevailing norms.
It mattered not to this fair one!
"Better this" she clearly said,
than living totally in black technology
with those who seem so dead!

# Special Pieces

If some new piano piece looks easy,
better assume it's not.
Melodies from The Greats often hadn't
the ready ease I sought.

Just take up and study a "childhood" book
and select something from Schumann,
then try to play "First Loss" and more,
to see why I carry on.

Or next take up the famed "Traumerie,"
and bend your will to that.
After I first tried, I soon set it aside
because it left me flat.

There're some pieces that no matter what
I try or how I labor
or how many hours I work on them,
no ease I ever savor.

So in disgust and disappointment
I banish them from sight,
to try another–then comes one
without a vicious fight!

Some music seems to fit my hand
and my fingers soon obey,
then soon enough I'm satisfied
with a special piece to play.

# Everything

Put everything on the line
as if life depended on it;
play the way you breathe and move
in action or as you sit.
Inhale in, but exhale more
and prepare what you wish to say;
lift your thoughts as you lift your hands
to the keys you're going to play.
Then worry not if a note or two
"ghosts" or falls short or flat.
Your goal is just to listen well
then play from your *habitat:*
"An array of resources," so they say,
"supporting survival and reproduction."
And so, your piano supports your life
and weaves a dream well begun.

# Memorizing

Sometimes my memory seems to fail
from one day to the next,
and then in protest I will wail–
so futile! I am perplexed.
Why do I "have it" for one day
then lose it? I'm so vexed!

It seems that I must then repeat
the passage two days in a row.
Measure by measure I creep along
from the start that I know,
then encounter the pesky phrase or two
that pure agony bestow
when they slip away from my mind,
and decide to just lay low.

No matter how much I try to play it,
be it fast or, oh, so slow,
it refuses the cleverest pitch I make
for the compliance I try to woo.
My memory has gone on vacation
refusing to return to the job,
requiring me to repeat and repeat it–
I'm just about ready to sob!

Again and again I start over
although I really try,
because I just cannot let win
this score even though I sigh.
I fancy myself a pianist, of sorts,
a rubric I can't let lie,
but must lift up my hands and head
and again–and again–just try!

# Murder on the Metronome Express

The only thing that surely keeps me
moored and not adrift at sea–
or murdering my trusty German metronome?
It's the beauty of his gorgeous teak wood!

So elegant in shape, a proud mini-pyramid,
he stands by the side of my *Duchess* so dear.
But when I hear the inexorable tick-tock,
my senses they go into terminal shock.

My hands start to quiver, my stomach does churn,
I'm sure this tempo lesson will never be learned!
I set it as instructed on the quarter value note,
and it starts off quite well 'til I go for broke,

Then all hell cuts loose and the rhythm does, too;
the phrase that was sound is followed by one to eschew.
It gets lost in mish-mash that I don't recognize;
to play with the General,* I completely agonize!

He reminds me of another, goose-stepping on high,
with one-two-three clicks–I think I will cry!
I hate marching orders and I've always rebelled.
What horrible fate on me just befell!

My teacher cajoles, exhorts, and then raises
promises and asks if I want piano praises
for possibly playing perfectly like a pro?
But what I really want is just to bed go!

———————
*Nickname I gave my metronome shortly after sighing,
then eventually agreeing to use it regularly in practice.

# No Mozart

I have no intention of playing Mozart–
not at the end and not at the start
of my senior experiment to relearn to play
lyrical pieces that transport me away
from the moment's demands of the provocative kind,
or traumas that ensue from the stress that I find
in life as it goes and unfolds in good time.
Ask not that I play pieces so fine
that most would believe no less than "divine;"
suggest not "La Mer," or "Fur Elise" by Mr. B.,
those old saws do nothing at all to please me.
So give me the Faun or the flaxen-haired girl
but no Claire of the Moon, though I love Debussy.

But yes! Tchaikovsky the man of "Swan Lake,"
or "Leibestraum" by the one of romantical fame
who wooed all the ladies with his arpeggios untamed.
R. Schumann's the man for whom I do swoon,
and Schubert's "Serenade" makes me cozy in cocoon.
Those I will play, and more of the same,
who approach melody to bring forth a song
that I will happily hum all the day long.

# The Returning Piano Student

The important duty of the pedagogue
is to teach us how to practice
(so says Gieseking the Great),*
to render the most satisfaction.

---

*Piano Technique by Walter Gieseking and Karl Leimer
(his teacher; originally published under a different title
in 1932; 1972 Dover edition). Walter Gieseking (1895-
1956) was a French-born German pianist and composer
renowned for his subtle touch, pedaling, and dynamic
control, particularly in the music of Debussy and Ravel.

(Though to learn he befriended Nazis
made me about ready to faint;
still his book was on my shelf.
Not read it? I really can't.)

I learned that scales are not required,
at least not by slavish practice,
but judiciously studied, along with etudes,
allows time to play the Classics.
So to improve I read about how
to become a piano virtuoso,
then thought some more about his point
on the teacher's proper role.

I decided that I differ somewhat
from the wisdom Gieseking offers,
at least when it comes down to me,
a returning senior who labors
to return to skills left far behind–
but not the depth of feeling
plus wisdom come from years of life
and reflection on their meaning.

A teacher's role is wider than
just giving us effective methods.
It's more to help us hear the tune
and understand the message,
then once heard and deeply felt,
they both will touch our heart,
and we know the reason to apply technique
with hope to create art.

# Professional vs. Amateur*

Though many come to an instrument
with a specific goal in mind,
to practice for a set event
and maximum confidence find,
along with perfection in technique
regarding tone or dynamic range,
then apply interpretation to readiness attain,
there are others who feel the love of music
and making it sing out,
who have no need to restrain that love
with limited time or thought,
no need to call forth our friendly muse
or send her off to bed,
saving then the best for last
with desire to turn a head.
For the "stage" of my piano dreams
has no audience around,
only my desire to pour music out
and express my love profound,
then please myself to well present
the gift the composer gave,
though no one listens–but perhaps they do
from their deep and soft, cool grave?
I play to acquit what I feel,
the respect I offer them,
the composers who began it all
and reign with diadem,
who never knew those of us
who give, no less than those
who honor music and the note
from a stage that's so remote.

------

*Inspired by articles by Frances Wilson, pianist, teacher, and
blogger on how professional vs. amateur musicians practice;
https://interlude.hk/on-letting-go-as-a-musician- part-1-letting go
of the music/, and interlude.hk/dedication-passion-inspiring-
world-adult-amateur-pianist/

We practice from the pure love of it,
to connect throughout the eons
and bring us closer to being One
with the Spirit to which we're drawn!

## Some Amusing Thoughts

I wonder if I shall petrify
before I get this right,
hand raised high in eternal hope
it'll come down on the note?
I wonder if I'll live to see
the very next Ice Age
before I mistress the right technique
to perform upon a stage?
I wonder if the cows will come home,
to happily chew their cud
before I put this Brahms to bed
without more piano blood?

———————

*Humor is a way I often get through practice, well
understood by an accomplished cellist, Janet Horvath;
https://interlude.hk/hilarity-onstage-classical-musicians
-funny-moments/?utm_source=mailpoet
&utm_medium=email&utm_campaign=Newsletter_22_Jul_2022

## Adult Learners

It's a horse of a different color
to teach an old dog new tricks, you know,
and shape musical dreams of her promised land.
It's the cat's meow if you can show
how reading scores first for structure and sound
works better than diving into rubato.
Her enthusiasm abounds, sometimes out of hand
and she often puts donkeys before carts;
needs help with music theories so confusing,
but will do her best, with all of her heart!

## Not Linear

I just read that progress in playing a piece
on the piano is surely not linear,
yet I used to think that once I rehearsed
that part, 'twas certainly all clear.

But then I read that that's not true!
One can resolve a problematic phrase
then the next day or days after that
it'll return to the original haze.

The same thing happens in how I memorize
a piece I've set my mind to;
I'll get it one day then lose it the next
then have to cement it anew.

That's just like life, as I think on it,
nothing goes in a straight line.
We bob and weave but then must repeat
if success we hope to find.

## Thoughts of a Piano Teacher

She's a virtuosa in the making,
while her soda bread is baking;
she first practices her tempo,
then goes on to knead dough,
but in both, I think she's faking.

# The Medication Solution

I may need a Valium
or an Ativan would do.
Perhaps a Prozac?
But a Mary Jane would, too,
to prepare me for my lesson
on my trusty piano,
though the lessons on rhythm
go agonizingly slow.
I may need a fan
or a pillow for my head,
after a rhythm struggle
when I wish I were dead,
feeling I'll faint or I'll cry,
or fall down on the floor
and kick and then scream
to even the score
with my teacher, though he's
usually quite jolly,
as I pursue my folly
to learn some more basics
and just how to play–
after what? No less than
a 63-year delay!

## Illiterate?

To love art "is to be illiterate,"
some teachers feel at base,
rather than encourage us to express
feelings they would erase.
A slippery slope if we are asked
to do more than analyze
musical theory, harmonics, and the like;
from the personal some teachers shy.
But accuracy's not the sole goal to teach
and besides, by whose definition?

Of course, that's needed, but not all
inherent in sound teaching.
For imagination and expression,
the stuff that feeds our soul,
combined with thought and then reflection
will a true artist then unfold.

## The Errant Student

To control an errant student,
stubborn as the erstwhile mule
(she balks, then does just what I ask
if I sit patiently as my main tool),
I must let her go a-meandering
through a piece that strikes her soul*
and suggests coming angel's wings
in future glories that be told,
then perhaps she'll let me guide her
and learn tempo to a "T,"
next with these skills she'll really soar
after I agree to teach this piece!

————
*Inspired upon hearing Grigori Sokolov play
Rachmaninoff's "Largo" from *Ten Preludes Op. 25.*

## Teacher versus Friend

A teacher is always a teacher
with a plan and goal to lend,
a friend is something different,
true to the bitter end.

A teacher wants to impart
and share expertise in love,
while a friend will hold your hand
but without the distant glove.

A teacher went before
and you're always aware of that,
but a friend will never ever
desert and leave you flat.

A teacher may talk down
and enjoy a lofty position,
while a friend is the same as you,
sharing both sadness and the fun.

They say a teacher comes
when we're ready to take a spin,
but a friend is always there,
with us through thick and thin.

So which is best you ask?
That's not a relevant question;
each serves a purpose for our souls
to feel ultimate satisfaction.

## Ode to an Ideal Piano Teacher

You are the Job to my desire,
your patience soothes and talent inspires.
You're the gentle rain upon my fire,
you teach me ways to pluck my lyre
and sing my song on my sweet *Duchess*.

You ride the waves of my "Texas"*
and teach me how to cowboy up.
You calm me down when I act up,
with ears open so that you hear
the songs that I do so revere.
You know just how to have me adhere
to your suggestions that are crystal clear.

You have the strength to push me on,
born of experience but not of brawn,
but most of all as we move along,
you respect what seems to be my song
and aren't "above" laughing with me,
no matter what I find of glee.
You're the right teacher I can plainly see;
the time is now, my desire is free!

———

*This reference seems particularly apt considering
the facts that I was born and raised early-on in
Texas, and that on some occasions during some
lessons, I fall into a blue or obstreperous mood!

58

# On The Duchess

♪♫♪

"I'm an interpreter of stories. When I perform it's like
sitting down at my piano and telling fairy tales."

– Nat King Cole

Fig. 7   Ann's favorite position from which to listen to Joe play
*The Duchess.*

A little bit of poetry, a little bit of doggerel,
should I contain myself?
I should and really ought-a!
But resisting's not my forte,
no matter what I try,
so sit back and relax,
but please, please do not cry!
There's much I want to say to you,
a lot I want to cover,
and thank you for support you gave,
and me with love did smother
and hold my hand and urge me on.
To compare there is no other:
I love you as my friends, my mentors,
and angels like my mother!*

———————

*I suspect my mom attended my party on June 18, 2022 because
she first instilled my love for music by purchasing a lovely 1953
Baldwin Acrosonic spinet, *Ms. Bellamy*, plus five years of lessons.
After my1928 Steinway M grand piano came to live with me, I
kept and occasionally play my spinet. I played my new piano at
my party, then Joe joined in by playing his favorite pieces, but
neither of us "performed." We preferred to relax and share our
deep love of music. Then I named my piano: *Rhapsody-Arabesque,
DMB (The Duchess of Music and Bliss).*




This is not a night for perfection,
but a time for reflection
and being with friends who share
a love for music, but without care
for other than what inside we hear,
without barrier, strife, or fear
that from our ego emanate.
So rest in peace and wait
for your inspiration should she come,
and play or express solely from love.

# Rhapsody-Arabesque, DMB

A rhapsody is a work, free-flowing in structure,
one movement long in contrasting moods and color,
an air of inspiration, a turn on a dime,
free in her form yet integrated in time.

An arabesque is ornamental, a melody unfolding
so freely, it seems slowing in time,
a curving moment like circular phrases,
not at all like the concerto with its structured line.

And so my *Duchess* is a right proper lady
with her sleek hair and dress of gorgeous red-gold,
ready at my call to help me express
eternal melodies that live in my soul.

# My Pledge of Piano Allegiance

I pledge allegiance to *The Duchess*
and to the love for which she stands;
I'll hold her tight,
practice with all my might,
and not forget my piano friends!

# Treasures

All that glitters is my piano,
my beautiful golden girl,
all that thrills are her ivory keys
and the melodies they unfurl.
All that carry me aloft
are the dulcet songs she sings,
the sweetest tone and touch has she,
so bright, the treasures that she brings!

# I Heard My Piano Play!

There was one day I heard my piano play,
not by herself, but along with me.
I swear I did!
Just once it happened since she came to live with me,
but when it happened
I almost fell off the bench.
The sound snuck up on me mid phrase,
rocked my soul, put me in a daze.
I heard her speak in tandem, as it were,
another voice in harmony with me.

An overtone? Perhaps, but I heard more.
The sound came out the open lid
to her strings, through which the soundboard sings.
I heard her join in with what I played,
but speak in a different voice,
fuller and richer than I'd heard to date.
I completed the phrase, but in a haze,
wondering what I had heard?

An ear mirage? A twin of my *Duchess* dear?
I fear I'll not hear it again because I haven't.
Yet I hope that won't be the case.
Someday again, when I'm relaxed and unaware
of other than just the music there,
she'll come to visit once more
and sing along with me in perfect harmony!

# The Difference

I love practicing on *The Duchess* now–
it's more like playing,
not work or a job!
I don't tend to sob so much
or shy away from taking on things
that seemed like pain before.

It wasn't that I didn't love
my spinet; yes, I did–and do!
But what my new piano gives
is a different stroke, a broader range,
a firmer touch, a wider tone
that lives between the white and black;
my spinet has some lack in that.

Now I venture outside the lines
from time to time,
keeping tempo as I must
in trust *The Duchess* will sing a richer song.
She's to opera as *Bellamy* to Broadway,
she's a starry night to a bright day.
Her voice so clear rings out
when I ask to be blessed
by her starry kiss!

## One Piano

There is only one piano for me,
not two or twenty,
this smiling, gorgeous girl
with strawberry curls
so free, and lovely curves
that captivate me.

And when she smiles
and beckons me,
her ivory pearly keys
do blind me to any other beauty
besides this one, this gift,
who often makes me weep
to hear her sing, and then allow
my touch, her silky skin so soft,
I dare not press too hard or leave a mark
or she might fall apart!

I courted her so long, it seems,
and waited for her comely tone
and lovely presence that
I only hoped would be.
And then—she was! At home at last,
and to my musical bosom
*The Duchess* I did clasp.

# A Good Addiction

So she's an addiction?
Well, she's *my* addiction, this piano of mine!
Standing so fine through eons of time
she's mine to have and play and fret
and try my best to get the softest softs,
the longest longs, so I can make my song
sing without a shout, but whisper fine
just like this rhyme, so natural a bent.

My soul is lent to her endeavors now,
not mine. Memories fade away of times past
that did not last. These do,
or at least this shoe fits.

Transported I within this endeavor,
try then try again but cannot push a lever
to make her sing!
But I can coax her ring if I attend with care
and do not try to snare her song in concrete.

I must be discrete, devoted, too,
to lessons learned 'til fingers burn
with practice, so that on her I can bestow
my love and complete devotion.
Quite a romantic notion!

# On Life

♪♫♪

"People profess to be lovers of music, but for the most part they give no evidence in their opinions and lives that they have heard it. It would not leave them narrow-minded and bigoted."

– Thoreau, Journal,<br>August 5, 1851

Fig. 8   A late December day just before baby's First Christmas
and before piano practice and a lesson.

# Iteration in the World of Pianos and Life

Life is an iterative* process.
We try, we learn, we try again,
each try just one step closer
to the perfection we imagine.

This process inheres in the musical world
for practice or presentation—
none are perfect from the start
if we fall prey to distraction.

The choice is ours to make
to get back on the horse,
or nurse our wounds or sit and sulk
or blame someone, of course.

'Tis grace we know, and good fortune, too,
that contribute to how we fare,
our powder kept dry even though we cry
still needs that basic flare.

It's effort's required and patience, too,
with allegiance to eternal hope,
but remember iteration and then we know
with all else we can cope!

---

*Inspired when my therapist, Cary Ann Rosko, listening to
me lament the months it took to publish my first poetry
book, commented that publishing is an "iterative" process.

## Values

What we value is what we do—
it's never what we say.
This I learned a long time ago,
as sure as the light of day.
So when I read Gregerson's book,*
she got it wrong I knew,
to ask the question: what do you like
that hasn't been ruined by you?

For what we value (the same as love)
is exactly how we behave.
Judge a person by how they treat
a person from the trades,
and seldom listen to just the words
that usually are just clack;
'tis only promise when we speak,
but reality when we act.

———
*From Linda Gregerson's poem "Not So Much
an End as an Entangling," in *Canopy*.


## Love at First Heart

Some believe in love at first sight,
an earth-shaking seizure of body and soul
that takes us on flight beyond gravity
into the universe as wonders unfold.

Some say love is only a chimera,
a relentless mirage or illusion of old,
that all love does is mislead by its deed
of hiding the truth from the smart and the bold.

Yet those brave enough to take up the challenge
might find that what's right will prevail.
As Maya Angelou said about the act of flying:
to do so requires taking the chance to fail.

## My Thanks

To those who allow me to draw
quite close to my essential being,
see the force within
that drives me now
to be just who I dream,
who show me the foundation
of a soul connected to
my song expressed without,
who hold up a mirror to reflect right back
what I aspire to be at heart–
to those valued friends,
without one doubt,
you have my love in full.
May your life be long and happy, too,
same for those whom you love, for sure!

## My Musical Friends

I have some friends whom I love to meet
every now and then,
because I feel such respect
for kindness shown without neglect.
They note the best that they see,
especially my musicality.
So I thank them each, my erstwhile friends
who share my song without an end
and blend their lives with mine sometimes
in lovely musical pastimes.

# The Lesson

Time will tell, give all things and
taketh away, in someone's time,
not mine.
The more we pine,
the farther things move away
from our wants, burning or just started;
martyred we, upon those coals of hot desire.

But give in, give up, and recede
and rest at ease after request,
then all that's best may come;
as Mick J. said,
if you try, sometimes
you'll get what you need.

Hold on to hope or all is lost!
Of that I'm very sure;
but the times in life I've wanted most,
I've lost.
Ask, then forget. Let the goddess
deliver; forget cost.
There's grace in not expecting,
more than blessing if there's getting,
and if not, there's love.

## Sometime in the New Year

Sometime in the New Year
should a soft breeze give you hope for spring
and a thought of me comes drifting by,
remember that I thought of you who warm my heart
and I held hope that you cared
what I thought and how I dared to speak my truth,
though sometimes we disagreed, never mind.
What binds is what we both know:
how music brings us wings to fly and more.

Sometime in this life,
should a tear come to your heart,
you may remember with a start
that I thought of you
and how you added to my life
and we flew high on musical wings,
mine new out of slumbering dreams,
your's you since days gone by.

A crystal sky, a scent of jasmine's bliss,
sunrise, sunset, nothing amiss
as we both knew, when reeling from the
music that we hear and feel,
we remember.

## Style

Some people sit and think,
others love to speak up and out,
some whisper thoughts in private,
others with their truth must shout.

Some prefer the silence sweet,
sitting peacefully alone
and careful to decide
when the heart may safely show.

No matter what your style
and no matter your clear preference,
if we focus on the meaning,
then no one will take offense.

None will feel beside themself,
a traitor to their mold,
yet two will surely join
in holding fast to one shared soul.

## Tsunami

A well-earned exhaustion we feel,
being oneself without apology
as some believe we are
and in the life ahead we'll be.
Add a pat on our backs for sure,
for surviving work and family
and singing our mellifluous song
as we lived through life's tsunami.
If we hope and waste no time,
a sweeter cause cannot be
than to go full-stop for glee,
though life is never carefree.

# Awe

We lose awe along the way.

Many things conspire to take it far away.
One could mention technology and how it plays
our lazy self against our better judgment.

Never wiser than the day we're born—or more awed!
Full of wonder and simple needs
that, easily expressed, are easily read.
But then we learn to obfuscate,
forget the words, ignore the sounds,
and let the mind bind our wearied souls
and others tell us what to hate
or who to love.

Above all, we lose wonderment along our way:
forget the thrill of early romance,
our first dance, the way a rose emits perfume
that leaves us in a trance.

If lucky, later we recall (vague memory at best)
just who we are. We struggle then to divest
ourselves of what others have said is "best" for us.
One layer at a time, the babe returns.
No books were burned
for this truth told, and may I be so bold to tell you
without one doubt:

*You know it all,* hold all the cards,
and though it's hard, you can backtrack,
remember all, let go, and be reborn.

------

*Inspired by a random though while floating in the alpha state
during a November 19, 2022 Chi Nei Tsang session with my
remarkable practitioner, Lisa Johnson, and reflected in this
statement by F.M. Alexander: "Re-education is not a process of
adding something but of restoring something."

## By Then

We know all when we are born,
the perfect brain and body, spirit, too,
then we iterate. But with luck
in the time when time speeds past,
the clouds part some, a beam of sun
of what we were comes through
and we remember who we are.
Parents fall away, we come out to play
again, and when it rains,
our suit is waterproof by then.


## Briefly

We live briefly, Mary Kelly* says;
our mothers likely said the same,
but our fathers left unsaid.
"What's life?" she asks,
and takes to task those who pursue
the rollback of our rights
as women.
Lint-based artworks she now displays,
filtered through the dryer's haze
of domesticity.
Not free,
though we struggle so to be.
Lint is our voice disappeared,
some might fear, but not so.
Chop and remix, expect redux,
repeat, relive-
but do not give in!
Live!

————

*Mary Kelly is a pioneer feminist conceptual artist
featured in "Time Again" by Sopjie Haigrey,
*New York Times Style Magazine,* November 13, 2022.

## Weakened

I am weakened and left a shell
of a former self. Is this hell?
Or is it heaven when I dissolve
into myself? Please, do tell!

I ponder a small number
of key questions on my mind,
like, how comes this true—if it does,
that what we wish is truth we find?

In thinking more what's in store,
if I understand the words I speak,
the positive adds color to a troubled world
we oft find dark and bleak.

## How We Do It

How silly then, will be the man
who robs himself of experience,
seeking rules and a safety net,
forgetting about excitement.
And clueless, too, the woman, she
who denies her flights of fancy,
opting instead to seek the "expert"
rather than be free.

The both of them, so sad
when they miss the mark so far,
the net not safe nor leading to
a self-expressive art.
Takes both the rule and then
to exercise free choice,
the balance of them both required
to achieve the goal of joy.

# Not Allowed!

It is not allowed
that we give up.
Death cannot be let proud
to claim us now,
because we do not give up!
We look up,
surely sigh, no doubt of that.
But give up?
No way of that!

It is not allowed
that we sit down.
We cannot drown
in the morass of crass
and lies and hate.
Wait! Yes, we weep
and sing a painful dirge
for what we suspect is,
or might come our way.
But not dance?
No way!

It is not allowed
that we waste ourselves.
We are not trash.
Every day our last;
so quickly moments pass
if we choose sorrow
much less hate.
Despair be banished,
not allowed,
not followed–
go away!

It is not allowed
to reject love,
a connection felt and more.
We must allow,
grasp and feel right now, not later.
But for what?
That we dive below and deeper in
the gift we have,
and on others bestow
more of our truest selves—
the source of light and love.


## Not Allowed 2


Not allowed
to sit
on your butt
and *not* create.
Not allowed to
shrink in space,
give up your place
in this crazy world.
Not allowed
to gnash your teeth,
descend in grief
to a cold, dark place.
Your place is here,
your time is now.
You're the master of your fate;
now go!


Celebrate!

## Jealousy

Jealousy is not love
as some would clearly say,
but a mean approximation that
true love will delay.
One cannot approach freedom, then,
which is all love truly is,
without an understanding of
what relationship really is:
the will to go or the opposite,
the will to stay and play.
All falls in place if we understand:
let go, and they may stay!


## No Chains

I just want to love you,
not claim you or grasp you or maim you,
approach you and touch you and hold you,
and gently or boldly enfold you,
connect us with no chains around you,
and with open hand, same heart,
receive you.


## Get On

Do I sit still for hero, villain,
muse, or foe, or lover missing?
Of course, no!
Those who populate my world
do not compel it,
though lust or delight, they might propel it.
If motivated from within,
to then sit still would be a sin.
Get on then, smartly, with steady gait—
those others can just sit and wait!

## Once Upon a Time

There was a time I thought it so,
but that was a very long time ago,
that love lies in just one man,
(or later, woman), or as it stands,
that love is limited without one doubt
to romantic dreams or perhaps a shout.

Then goddess blessed me with true understanding,
when I awoke and started questioning:
*if I view love in limited quantity*
*or with just one definition as I believed,*
*why don't I think the same of emotion,*
*or intellect or spirit, as I hadn't done?*

Being me, a lady of a certain intellect,
(or wanting to show that desired aspect),
and devoted to living a life with pleasure,
and wanting more love, not less, to treasure,
how could I persist with such a view
consistent with unreason that I so eschew?

From that day on (I was at least twenty-five)
I vowed to live a happy life,
free of "ownership" and thoughts of less,
or limits in what would lead to bliss.
And so I have, not always successful,
but hoping I was kind, yet never dull!

## Wondering

I would really like to know if ever
he thought of me that special way?
And did he come unglued, undone,
and let soft feelings then hold sway?

Did he think of me at dusk or dark
when his day and chores were done,
or wonder just what could have been
before the warmth of morning sun?

Did he think of how it might have been
to reach across a distant mile
and take my hand or touch my cheek
and feel the contours of my smile?

## Knowing

There are a million yeses, just like shades of blue,
in how I think of you.
There are a trillion falling stars that alight
in the darkest of places,
reminding me in quiet times
that in my short life, no matter how long,
there are ways that souls connect,
eyes see, and we never do forget
those who touched us, but never knew.

What matters is that I knew. I felt you,
what might be in store, because I lust to be in this life
complete and whole but yielding to pure feeling
that leaves me reeling and wanting more.
There are a million tears that come to me
unbidden, yet I know are my due,
from the deepest kind of place, a space within
that you saw and knew.

# Libertine

To say that I'm a libertine
doesn't mean that I am crass.
To say that I'm a sexual being
doesn't mean that I've no class.
But men will often assume it's so,
then express themselves so brashly,
assuming that a free-spirited soul
means I'll descend to banality.

So boys, please think with much, much more
than what you sport below!
There's more than a body involved in me;
first touch my soul, you know,
then maybe, body might come along
if you also start with mind,
the three wrapped up in one full bundle
is the whole me that you'll find.

# Chances We Don't Take

What we grieve is what we imagine
could be, when souls blend,
the desire to be accepted whole
and forgiven all our sins.

Could be, too, when others are gone,
we really grieve the actual,
the things that connected in our lives
that can be counted as factual.

But what hurts most is when not seen
for who we think we are,
no reflection back of values held dear,
before our final *au revoir.*

I wonder if, when we meet again,
we'll have another chance
to this time take the time
to join in just one dance?

## To Understand

To understand someone
requires we step back and listen,
no less in life than music.
But more than listening is required
to a song or person whom we value:
an open mind, an open heart,
a willingness to hear.
It starts if you can but imagine
what I hold dear, how I suffered
and how I strove,
what was important and forward drove
my actions and my words.
What I hold dear derives from what I endured,
what I heard, learned, and felt
to play the cards that I was dealt.
If you hold me dear then you will hear,
and if you don't, you won't.


## Our Sole Song

It's so mysterious how
one touches the lives of others,
sometimes bidden, sometimes not,
when caught up in our imagination
and see ourselves reflected back,
on some occasions, as more than what it is:
a passing glance, kind word or two,
and we once more take flight
in pure delight to be "seen,"
then we conclude there's more, but are deluded
in finding what was not in store
with mere mortal men;
some not true friends,
but offering a friendly gesture or two,
and then life moves on
and we are left with our sole song.

# I Still Have a Beating Heart

I still have a beating heart.
I still break or shake
if you show me anger
when none is deserved.
Even if mainly reserved,
I tend to shrink from conflict,
at least until I can do no other
than screw up my courage
and then the bother to
face down my demons
that have arisen and will not let go.

In those circumstances
I cannot just look away
and ignore what I feel
and let it fester there,
because it will not let go
until I go there, and deal with it,
first, by confirming what I value
in what you kindly gave to me
by way of support, if not love,
and lastly, confirming the above.

But then I must speak my truth,
express how I feel—nothing rational
to be sure—then ask for what I'd like.
Your response of course, not mine to make.
My risk? I won't be heard, no change in store,
but the major chore has been done,
the final chord properly played
when I conclude with kind words said,
then go my way, relieved of burdens of restraint.
Removed at last, the scar of taint
allows, for me, the sun to shine
as peace and happiness again are mine.

# M. J. A.

It's easy to miss someone in life,
but harder to be free;
the one who yearns cannot control
when the other wants to flee.
Though you may desire a different fire
when someone's your nominee
but his life moves on and he is gone,
then you're a refugee.
"Everyone goes off the freeway,"
a friend once said to me.
"Could be long or could be short...
You'll live, though he set you free.
Real freedom then for you to find
is to use the true passkey:
every cloud a silver lining has,
just look and you will see
that peace comes from deep inside.
It's something the gods decree:
the secret is to let him go
and you choose to be free."

If you ever fear to fail,
just know that you will not.
The courage it takes to live
is something you've already got.

If you think you're not enough,
that you better give much more,
know you've touched many lives
with your kindnesses galore.

If you ever want for more
or just a special thing,
look at the friends you have
and treasures that they bring!

## The Edge

Trip lightly on the razor's edge,
look down the empty barrel,
there's danger that inheres within
these things if you're not careful.

Next question if perhaps, perchance
it's right, if we feel safe
when sharing thoughts in privacy,
then a chance, it's worth to take?

But one must move and must not wait
or life will pass on by
and take us to our graves alone,
a loss, and then a sigh.

## Some Kind of Love

I write you poems in my head.
The moment's here and then it's dead.
No words remain, they've flown the coop,
and though I try, I cannot recoup
the thought 'twas there, so I just stare
and then allow the shower's magic
to envelop me in reverie.

Warmth does infuse and calm the mind,
vague memory of something kind,
like strings of harp are plucked sometimes.
The air's perfumed with lemon rinds,
plumeria's bloom that came too soon
and died away, leaving to play in mind
the memory of some kind of love.

Disruption in the world,
no less than in relationships,
from rude behavior on our streets
to war that does life eclipse,
from random killings in our schools
or rape and pedophilia,
sex trafficking or domestic violence
by misogynist or cave man,
comes when we know not how to feel
then clearly self-express
with hugs, soft words, or what we create,
then others we'll transgress.

If our passions don't release with art
and love and true compassion,
they'll smolder then incinerate
and we'll soon be undone.

But more than just compassion's needed:
to empathy we must hold fast.
If I can't imagine how you feel
then all is lost at last.
What else lies beneath all bad behavior,
destroys all for which we've striven
and threatens both victim and the perp?
All is values driven.

If we don't value human life
above gold, that's one great sin,
or value health and independence
to the extent that freedom's given,
if we don't act by word and deed
to support what we hold dear
and try to live it every day,
then into hell we've crawled, I fear.

# Kudos to the Writer Cleary

Me, a troublemaker? Not like Beverly
(Cleary, that is), no pushback I displayed;
perhaps I needed her chutzpah to resist
a mom who told her that she'd "fade?"

Yet Cleary, a stubborn girl instead–
and a hearty huzzah I say to her!–
went on to map kids' inner lives,
a lifelong pot that she did stir.

Though she often felt "rebellious"
and also "angry" and "guilty,"
she opposed the silly adult world
of "cold, foreign, and arbitrary."

So kudos, Cleary, I admire you plus
your fictional character, Ramona Quimby:
fiery, sloppy, creative, and loud,
proud, and quixotic. Hear! Hear!

---

*Inspired upon learning about the death of
writer Beverly Cleary (1916-2021) in an article
by Sam Anderson, *New York Times Magazine*,
December 28, 2021

# Ready to Retire*

What tipped the boat over
that you decided to move over
and out and allow someone else
to thrive or suffer or whatever one does
when working for The Man?

Jump in—it's fun to swim!
Take a chance on the chance you'll love it!
Tell that boss to just go "shove it"–
walk out the door–no, run out
then shout "I'm free" to just be me!

("Oh wait...I've got to figure out
how to 'be me' now that I'm free...
But so be it; I'm done, I'm gone,
I'm on to something new.
For sure I'll happy be,
to feel so free to just be...me!")

———————
*Inspired when my friend J.B. told me he
was ready to retire.

## Real or Imagined?

Our brain fills in what we perceive,
or at least we think we do,
a missing link we imagine there*
when the "fact" is just not true.
The Ponzo illusion is an example
of how our eyes deceive.
Other examples prove this well:
how often perceptions mislead.
Curious examples to be sure,
and some are truly sad,
like times I took a word or two
and extrapolated what was said,
then readily led in my fertile brain
to a state so easily aroused,
with passions awakened in my head
and thoughts of love so readily caused.

Flights of fantasy and poems ensued
connecting all the lines,
inventing an interest that wasn't there,
encouraging me to be blind
and journey alone among the stars
and read their every word,
seeking out what I wanted to hear
in pursuit of the absurd.
The notes I readily added to
the score they might have played,
were melodies I thought I heard
but in truth, were not displayed.
A moment only, but not to be,
a connection no deeper than
one short moment that I shared
with these real–or imagined friends.

———
*"Be careful of something that's just like you want it to be" from
"I've Always Been Crazy" by country singer Waylon Jennings;
what he said! Parasocial relationships with media stars and
influencers are an example.

# What is "Beauty"?

Is beauty "a love charm that's doomed to expire"*
and does it run skin deep?
Does feeling lovely depend on definitions of
the company that we keep?

Is what's left after a crashing concerto
of the most artistic notion,
nothing more than ashes after fire
in the greatest conflagration?

How fast we forget the mighty Phoenix
who burned in what some consider
a tragedy and a loss of all
in a paroxysm of pity.

But rise not we up, we women of spirit
to rail against the stupid
who narrowly focus on the surface,
and not what's clear within?

For what is beauty, let not men define,
nor women totally imprison
in a judgment that remains skin-deep
but with truth is in fatal collision.

So what is "beautiful" I often recall,
what brings me ultimate pleasure,
is knowing that I'm complete and whole
in the beautiful me I treasure.

———————
*Statement of a feminist author, quoted in *A Left-handed
Woman: Essays* by Judith Thurman.

# This Alone Would Make One Tired!

I think I'm about to get tired and "old"
from society's age prejudice!
I read that 76 is an "advanced" state
In AARP's *Bulletin*, no less.

I guess that's better than a few years ago
when I just about fell over
to read a reporter's clear implication
that I should be pushing clover.

About a crime committed, she said
that an "elderly" person was attacked,
yet the victim was 54-years of age
and a mere youngster at that.

Perhaps I should amend my book's back cover
to stress the remarkable feat
that I restarted piano lessons once again
as an "elderly" person–so neat!

Should I deserve a Piano Medal of Honor
for persisting in expressing myself
after re-finding music at my "advanced" stage?
Should I already be on the shelf?

So when do we "age" and what should we expect
when as "seniors" we feel quite young?
We've bitten the bullet and made our contribution,
but aren't seen for the good we've done.

Bury not your head in the sands of youth;
your time will come for sure.
Speak up against prejudice that seems never to have
a solution or possibly a cure!

# Strange

We're the strangest beings, are we not?
complex and paradoxical,
eccentric, demanding, and ridiculous,
quixotic, and egotistical!

Often obtuse or strongly opinionated,
and subject to our times,
and how we were raised and what was praised
that stuck within our minds.

But then there's more as there always is,
the black has white, the rain, rainbow.
It takes a friend to remind us when
under life, there's an eternal flow.

Beauty walks the world, but needs eyes to see,
a remembering day-to-day,
our weariness only sometimes overcome
by a friend's kind touch today.

By that we know to just let go
and dwell within what we value:
kindness, respect, curiosity, and love–
the things we already knew!

# What I Would Like to Hear

Some things I'd love to hear from a man–
may I, without judgment or strife–
things that I don't believe
I've often (ever?) heard in my life?

1. "I'm sorry I said that, I truly am;"
2. "I'm sorry that happened to you;"
3. "There's no excuse for what I did then;"
4. "I'll speak up if it happens again;"
5. "I understand what you say and felt;"
6. "That wasn't fair, my love.
I'll do my best to do much better
to defend you the very next time;"
7. "Take your time, you look great,
that damn party on us can wait!"
8. "I'd love to go clothes shopping with my One,
and help you choose from your try-ons."

Then what I'd like never to hear again,
at least, not in this lifetime,
(but I won't hold my breath nor count what is left
if a connection is never aligned):

1. "I'm sorry that you feel that way, my friend"
(no apology for his behavior
or recognition of how he offended);
2. "Can you please get to the point right now?"
3. "I'll solve your problem" (and his!) he says;
4. "Can I help you with dishes, my love?"
(as if the bloody dishes are mine);
5. "I got you a new skillet, my dove"
(as if I own cook-things divine!).

# To My Women Friends

I find (don't you?), that many men
get tired of helping you,
especially to understand something new
you'd like to, or when you ask
too many questions,
then their patience runs thin,
and they defend a short answer
by telling you you're "overwrought"
or really "making a mountain out
of a just a molehill."

That could be true—but for me, not.
If it's understanding that I sought
and seek when I find a topic
that I want more than to peek inside,
but truly understand,
then why suggest or tell me that my quest
is silly, or imply that I'm quite dim
to not understand what you say
quite as fast as you would, I pray,
or I give it more importance than you would
because you already understand the topic
and perhaps think that, also, I should?

Such judgment I eschew,
though you may not see my point.
If time is scare or you'd rather not
delve into the answer
or if you think I'd better learn
to search elsewhere or on my own,
just tell me that—don't leave me flat,
replete with unanswered questions
not complete—not yet,
but with my confidence perhaps shaken.

But hey! No offense taken.
I know how to get just what I need,
and usually it resides, at least partly so,
in taking my quest to women friends
who, in the end, have patience galore
to spend what time they have,
helping me grow in understanding
of what I wish to know
without telling me the mountain does not exist
in what they perceive of as a mole.


## No Mystery About Women

Why can't men tell me how they feel,
or apologize? (Women will laugh at that!)
Don't fix me, if you please,
just listen. (Women will laugh at that!)
Don't look away if you offend,
but look at me. (WWLAT)
There's no offense taken if I just "want to talk,"
but there sure is, if you walk away.
Don't explain if I complain (shall I say it again?).
Just sit still and look at me and listen,
then apologize, if need be.
We're really quite simple,
and it's no mystery what we want:
to be seen, to be heard, and to know
(at least once in a blue moon)
what you feel, not think.
Then kiss me quick, be on your way;
we'll live to love another day!

# *Donne* *

*Donne*–we are all women, true!
(What did my mother mean
to say, "We women suffer so"?
From that, what do I glean?)

We weep, we laugh, we know our truth–
then forget it in a flash.
Come clash and clang of prison gates
and we're alone at last.

The worm that's buried, oh, so deep,
propels us to *one* fate;
it's sinuous, slimy, seductive self
tells us it's "too late."

So will it cause us to be silent
or seduce our mortal sin
to let love and art and music, all,
retreat to live within?

———

*Donne*, Italian for "women." Inspired by the website of
opera singer Gabriella di Laccio, https://donne-uk.org
di Laccio's mission is to make more visible the prodigious
contribution of women to music. She reports the astounding
and devastating fact that, in October, 2022, almost nine out of
ten pieces played by orchestras around the world were composed
by white men. She provides a list of more than 5,000 women
composers, and offers program consultation services to music
directors who are committed to the inclusion of women, including
minority and LGBQT women, in order to achieve a more just
musical world.

# "Stupid" versus "Criminal"

Not intending to preach
as I'm sure that you know,
only intending on you
a few laughs to bestow.

I don't know about you
but clearly true for me,
Cipolla's* definition of stupid
surely causes glee:

"Stupid" hurts all others
but at the same time
has no benefit to "stupid,"
no reason and no rhyme.

At least the criminals have
the chutzpah to steal
and derive a benefit–
now that's the real deal!

So for "stupid" they deserve
all of what they get,
but criminals, they have
my nod of deep respect.

———
* *The Basic Law of Human Stupidity*, by
Carlos M. Cipolla (1922-2000) provides a
masterful, hilarious definition of "stupid"–
the best I have ever read! Cipolla, an Italian,
taught economics at the University of
California, Berkeley.

# Delirium

Booster* delirium knocked me to hysterium,
from there into dreamland and then to mysterium.
Better than t'other would say my mother.
I want out from bed covers, if I had my druthers!

———————

*The second anti-Covid booster knocked me for a loop!
The next night I slept 14 hours. Gratefully, side effects
were few and I'm glad I'm better protected now!

# About Anti-Vaccers

What I want is what I suspect
that you want, all of us the same,
to be accepted in full bloom,
allowed to be as we came
into the world. Just reflect back
the best of who I am and then
for me, all others and the world,
to create love again and again.
Allowing and reflecting, both must be
the secrets to a peaceful soul
at once more creative, with us fulfilled
and a history that can be calmly told,
not ruined with rot of those so desperate
who illogically (and stupidly?) choose to resist
what public health and science so clearly insist,
because they feel so out of control
and never, ever loved at all.
So will we survive the onslaught of this,
a wily virus that befalls those who live
and love right now, with our toils and all
the troubling trends? Depends on what
we give and do, and if love for others
prevails in the end.

## Inclusion?

The Olympics have finally come
to open up again,
let in break dancing as a game
with a golden prize to win.
Inclusion? Yes, they're on the path
to a wider appeal to all,
and tout the Paralympics to prove
they're woke (and lawsuit forestall?)

But are they really so very just
in who they invite to the games?
Consider this, the powers that be
refused to lend their name
to gay athletes, no permit to
say "Gay Olympics." How odd to note,
considering the source of games,
the Greeks of open sexual fame!

---

*In 1982 the U.S. Olympic Committee sued to bar a sports
event from using "Gay Olympics." The courts upheld this
claim; https://www.history.com/news/first-gay-games-olympics

## History

Social media, "often a corruption of our soul,"
then jumped to TikTok
where Beoncé dropped her...what?
So said the news reporter. So bold!
So perspicacious to note our foible!
What good, such wisdom
pontificated from a platform
by a reporter paid millions, several?
Yet youth still shoot,
birthed unwanted in the blood they pass on
and thrive or strive but suffer so.
Amazing how we repeat history
until we pass on.

## What Good?

What good to rue world politics
and leaders crazed or, oh, so slick,
the ones who live to others hate
or the ones who love to prevaricate,
the ogre seeking blood to let
or the devil maiming the innocent?
Spend no more on it than a moment's thought,
then move back to your own sane heart!


## On How to Deal With The TV News

I got ready, I did, to write you a poem
to tell you about my brand-new song
that I'm sharing with *The Duchess*,
with whom my efforts were blessed,
and then got waylaid by the news truly dismal,
so I had to stop dead and consider and mull
what I wanted to remember or hope or believe,
and if my angst at the news I could relieve?

I looked deeply inside and into my heart,
then thought about you, just as a start
in remembering all who lifted me up
or loved or supported, or with me did sup.
I'll hold tight to those thoughts that seem to be all
to avoid the depression into which I may fall
to do less that my very best, just today,
to create, to play, to listen–then pray.

*Pink*

I went up and put on the warmest of things
to remember the happiness that pink always brings,
a cozy little sweater, the softest of fluff
to stroke, like ivory keys of my dear *Duchess.*

But every now and then I revisited the thought
though I used my best efforts to destroy what it
brought:
how is it we seniors could live to be here,
a repeat of the 50s—we were already there!

Once lived, one might think the generations will learn
to enjoy and preserve all the freedoms we earned.
Apparently not so, though we aren't the ones
to build the funeral pyre* on which freedom burns.

---

*Built by Putin when he invaded Ukraine on February 24, 2022
and then threatened nuclear war.

# The Morning News on April 29, 2022

I'm not here this morning to ruin your day,
but I wonder if we should drop and pray?
I never thought I'd hear the news say
that we best consider a Nuclear Day!

The lessons of the Cold War must be forgotten,
warns a TV anchor about Putin's plan
to escalate the Ukraine war and signal his intention
to control all their land, next the lives of you and me?
Then for generations hence, how could anyone be free?

"Boy, that's troubling" the news anchor said,
when the professor predicted
more than what we imagine:
"almost nothing" at the center in many thousands dead
that the bomb plus fallout would cause in destruction.
She went on to tell us that a new album would drop
(was it by Adele or Jon Batiste or drill music? I forgot,
just like I'd like to remember this day–not!)

Do we live in the Valley of Insanity? We must!
A pornography more vicious
than brought on by just lust:
the destruction of others, of life, and our world.
He must be the devil to hell us did hurl.

Do not dwell on things you've done
or to you what others have done,
it's futile to regret the past
when the best is yet to come.

Do not fail to see it all:
the answer's always there;
it will come to you if you wait
the full time it takes to appear.

# The Supreme Horror

Increasing the domestic supply of infants?*
Using women as incubators for adoptable children?
Children as "product" to be managed and sold?
How about forcing slave women, as history's racist sin,
to bear children to increase the labor supply
or provide profit from children's sale, beyond bold,
as white masters did and only some now decry?
Let's call it what it is, the *Dobbs'* court decision,
one we should react to with more than derision:
"maximizing white male power
and consolidating wealth."
So says Michelle Goodwin,** no doubt her opinion.

So do we sit here in paralysis near complete?
Or translate into ire our abject depression,
first taking full stock of where we got to,
then finding our gumption to move in conjunction
and take away thrones of those who proclaim
they're "pro-life" but value the unborn above women,
rendering us nothing but vessels to birth
fascistic oppressors from Handmaid-like* semen?
We let down our guard and failed to take note
that extremists were working even while we slept
and moved back to the past more than 50 years
with us not realizing what tears would be wept.

---

*Inspired by horror of "The Handmaid's Tale," a novel by
Margaret Atwood, and in listening to the analysis of the
*Dobbs'* decision and one of Supreme Court Justice Alito's
rationales to strip away women's 50-year-old constitutional
right to abortion; https://www.youtube.com/watch?v=
zu9eCWrhMxg
**Professor of Law, University of California, Irvine

## Oklahoma *

If you live in Oklahoma, you now can sue
if a woman obtains an abortion you think abuses you.
Her and her doctor you want to control
because you won't banish the devilish troll
who seeks forever in rapture to abide
and take you along on a hellish ride
to abuse others. That's what's going on
and with such abuse, you so easily go along.

There's more than just pity on you to bestow.
We must stem the tide that threatens overflow
to suffocate us all as we drown in the venom.
We must take every step possible to exorcize him,
be it in lawsuits or shunning or even a hymn.

______

*On hearing about the law passed in Oklahoma on April 29,
2022 to allow anyone to sue a health care provider and any
woman who obtains an abortion.

## "Hysteria"?

Who knew I'd wax poetic about politicians
(though in politics is my bachelor's degree)?
I can't help but sound vitriolic against
former governor, Chris Christie.*
So from his pontificating platform he said,
an opinion women wouldn't find odd
(on Sunday morning's "This Week With George"):
'twas "manufactured hysteria" against *Dobbs*.**

So transparent the governor's sexist mindset,
just look back a few centuries at least,
to how men put women in lockdown, and worse,
some never to be released,
at least not from opprobrium heaped on their heads
by calling them "mentally deranged,"
to justify removing all of their rights,
with misery men's main aim.

So, wake up Mr. Christie! You're way behind times.
Or, perhaps a better solution will ring
if you won't step down because you're so blind–
when CBS does the right thing.

———

*Chris Christie is a lawyer and was former governor of
New Jersey from 2010 to 2018, and is sometimes a panelist
on CBS-TV's Sunday morning show, *This Week* with George
Stephanopoulos and is a candidate for President in 2024. He often
touts his credentials in "civil rights," but, apparently, in this 2022
statement, this does not include women.
**In *Dobbs* "The Supremes" overturned 50 years of women's
Reproductive rights to abortion.

"Our brains are breaking,"* our skin pulled back,
the sinuses stretched, eyeballs are slack,
entrails hang out and putrefy,
yet the NRA still tells us lies.
"Guns are the solution!" they falsely cry.
"Arm the teachers!" politicians answer,**
while some call–again–for patience and prayer.***
"Overwhelming grief," Obama said,
while mothers wept as their children bled.
Just ten short years from Sandy Hook–
"we'll surely do something in the aftershock!"
But the slaughtered babies' wispy souls
still stagger among us, their spirits roiled
and not at peace while we make war
and guns prevail over life–so bizarre!
Yet it's "not yet time to talk about change,
but time to grieve,"**** and hold hands
and come together, the gun-lovers claim?
Access to guns, ok, I'll agree,
but assault rifles used in most killing sprees?
Do deer wear Kevlar so ARs are needed,
then kids slaughter kids,
and the mayhem goes unheeded?

––––––––––

*How US Senator Chris Warner, Democrat, Connecticut,
responded on the Senate floor immediately after 19 fourth
graders and two teachers in Uvalde, Texas were slaughtered
by an 18-year-old boy on May 24, 2022.
**Immediate response to the slaughter by Republican US Senator
Ted Cruz and the State Attorney General from Texas; so much for
loving children over unregulated access to assault rifles.
***Then-President Obama's response to the 2012 slaughter of 24
children at Sandy Hook Elementary School in Newtown, CT.
**** What Republican US Representative (Uvalde District) Tony
Gonzalez said when on May 25, 2022, ABC-TV news commentator
Gayle King asked if it wasn't now "time for change?" N.B. that
King pushed back.

# Not My Texas

You force women to have babies
who they don't want–
obviously to provide targets
for the assault weapons you flaunt.
"Expect more, pay less"
must be your slogan,
since lives of the young
you need for your guns
in order to practice
the venom that you preach:
"Live free, own guns"
is the cant that you teach.

We're not your womb
to bear your kids,
they'll not be used
to ammo be fed,
nor are women your slaves
to loss of control you dread
and so impose your will
on whom you wish dead.

What else do you want?
Nothing it seems
but to take away life
and of youth, their dreams.
The slaughter of innocents
lies in your bed,
and with you in it
is a world that I dread.
It might be *your* America
but death's not my aim,
nor is Texas a birth state
I'll ever again claim.

The perfect example he surely is
of the quintessential cowardly hypocrite, as is
the Texas Governor. Forget not his name:
"Abbott"* will go down in infamy's flame,
born out of light and in darkness he came
for saying only that dead children
"are gifts we should love and support families"
whose loved ones they now grieve.

But as we know, the good governor who "cares"
so much about hearts shattered,
and "tears he does share" with people rightly angry,
says "we should not rip apart,
but come together and support each other with heart."

What's missing in this alligator-teared remark?
Certainly, no mention of banning assault rifles
or more regulation or banning ownership
by those with convictions or mental health problems,
or those under 18 of unsound mind and crime record.

The "problem" Abbott says, is the mental health surge
in Uvalde and Texas, no less than the world.
So for him it's easier to solve this grave problem
than regulate guns?** How absurd. How perverse.
How courageous Beto O'Rouke
who called out "no clothes"
on the elected Emperor of this retarded state.
How long will Texans support this outrage?

--------

*Abbott refused to support safe storage laws, expand Medicaid
that pays for mental health, and signed a law allowing permitless
carry less than two years after mass shootings in El Paso and
Odessa when a total of 30 people perished in outrageous carnage.
He signed laws giving teachers more access to guns in schools.
**The law allows most Texans to carry handguns openly in public
without going through training or having to get permits. Long
guns had already been allowed to be carried without a permit.

## The Real Solution to School Shootings

Please give this a go, Representative Gonzalez*
(who wanted to "grieve" while so many others bleed)–
here's the solution to reduce the slaughter of babes
or at least give the parents something to grieve:

Send kids to school dressed in Kevlar, the vest kind,
then their bodies you surely will find
when evil souls walk in and shoot heads off,
if you please,
with assault rifles they obtain with the greatest of ease.

At least then distraught parents can bury *some* remains
untouched by the profane destruction
that so easily came,
and you can persist to demand unfettered access
to weapons of war you hold tight to your chest.**

Thus, to continuing evil you join in testament
with your simpering and whining
and obscene pronouncement.

---

*What Republican US Representative Tony Gonzalez of Texas
(Uvalde District) said a day after the mass slaughter on May 24,
2022 of 19 children by an 18-year-old boy using an AR rifle.
**ABC-TV news commentator Gayle King asked, but Gonzales
said it wasn't time to change, only to grieve. N.B. that King pushed
back; https://www.theguardian.com/usnews/live/2022/may/
25/texas-school-shooting-news-victims-uvalde-elementary-school-
latest-updates

## Two Labyrinths

There are many mornings when I disappear
into the Labyrinth of Music.
Sitting alone at my breakfast table
listening to sonatas sweet or strong,
oft times my body joins my mind
and chills run down my spine
as the ruder points of life escape my notice
and I could go on the same, all day long.
But on some days like today,
the fateful third hearing
of the Senate Select Committee
to explore "chump's" attempted coup,
the chills, they come for reasons of a darker kind,
the kind that tells us that in "open and plain view"
our former president plans to try another coup
and take all power that the majority did eschew
when we voted him out of office
as was his just reward from such untoward acts
of fomenting violence of the physical kind
with untrue words he lent to the rioters' cause.

He must atone! But more so disappear,
perhaps into another labyrinth of a different kind,
Lower down in the hell he deserves
to use his Big Lie to egg thugs on
and attack all patriots of the real kind,
those who believe in law
and power of the legitimate kind.

---

*Testimony June 22, 2022 of conservative former federal circuit
judge J. Michael Luttig, who fears for the fate of American
democracy and the republic if "chump" or a supporter loses the
2024 Presidential election.

## *Humanity?*

"Where is the humanity?"
a question asked on the news*
seeing a prisoner, nearly dead from a crash
he went through,
then dragged from the van, prone and unresponsive
into a police station, then to his cell,
head clearly dangling.
Like a puppet doll he was, to life barely clinging;
how can we bear it to see him treated this way?
Or ignore the harm caused from pure hate on display?
"Where is the humanity?" I ask you again.
What kind of country do you want to live in?
"The Supremes" ripped away a constitutional right,
50-years of reproductive freedom;
full misogyny in sight.
Of a sudden the unborn have far more rights
than the women who in some states
must give up their life
bearing unwanted children offered up
as victims of gun rights?
"There's a lot of pain" she declared.**
Ya' think so, Ms. King?
Thinking on the results that Putin's bombing does bring
to the remarkable, resilient,
beyond courageous Ukraine.

---

*Question asked on June 29, 2022, CBS-TV's *Mornings* by reporter
Tony Docoupil. He was responding to horrific images in news of
multiple police officers in New Haven, Connecticut, dragging and
hackling Richard Cox (a Black man), who had been arrested on a
weapons charge. On the way to the police station, Mr. Cox was
severely injured in a crash, because the police transport van had
no seat belts. His head crashed into the back of the van during the
accident, rendering him paralyzed from the waist down. Police
officers at the station continued their inhumane physical treatment
and said that Mr. Cox was "not really hurt" and should "get up."
**Gayle King, also a reporter on CBS-TV's *Mornings*

Now Finland and Sweden finally move to join in
a NATO alliance they formerly disdained
when ignoring the chance that down war could rain.
Are some waking up? Is it too late to freedom save?

When does it end? The pain and the death?
The Beast, who now more than a head he does raise,
but moves limbs underneath him
and begins to stand up.
Then our creeping dread leads us to clearly see
what walking death can look like
in a world that was free.
But this country, now lost because freedom
we compromised, and democracy's dead meat
with "chump" and his allies.

# Adult or Baby?

Why do people snick and snigger
about anything sexual?
But then if someone's truly interested,
they readily join the chorale?
Why do most devolve into a heap
of giggles and derisive snorts
when the news discusses reproduction
or relations of the sexual sort?
The post-*Dobbs'* surge of vasectomies
reduced CBS newsmen to quivering.*
Asked one, "Will the caveman still feel OK?"
to engage in such impaling?

They writhed and wriggled in their chairs,
these grown manly men with children;
what message will they pass on to their kids
about real sexual education?
Yet in sex I'm sure they did indulge–
an experience for the most of us
the most human, joyful of activities,
yet to discuss it, they cause a fuss.

---

*The reaction of two CBS-TV's *Mornings* newsmen
on July 23, 2022, when they reported doubling of vasectomies in
the month after the anti-women Supremes stripped away women's
constitutional right to abortion. Many young and childless men
began opting to support women by exercising their (still-
existing) reproductive freedom, by making this simple in-office
ten-minute (often reversible) procedure with a typical two-day
recovery. So, too, can women opt for in-office sterilization by
laparoscopy. This is a simple procedure using a small light and
cauterization tool inserted through tiny incisions over and under
the navel. The procedure allows women to go home within hours
and typically with minimal side effects. I know; in 1972 at age 28
I opted to have one at the UCSF Medical Center when I was single,
childless, and certain I never wanted to have children. I have never
regretted that decision.

The Puritans live! So, too, the church
that sank its fangs in us,
and reduce us to jellied jellyfish
when sex we deign to discuss.

What kind of chains did we accept?
How willing we are to give in!
How long will society act so stupid
because some think sex a sin?

## Age

When we get old
we talk of how age brings wisdom
in perspective given
on how we look at life
and what we see or find important.
Could be.

'Tis true, there's a winnowing down
to just the bones of it,
no time for cant,
no patience for the confused.
Think first, speak clearly,
or do not abuse my time
for there is little left.

If you don't lean left in politics
please pass me by, or you, I will.
I won't be anybody's shill for intolerance
nor waste my time trying to convince you to be free.
One thing I do know and see so clear:
I feel when there's a heart, or not, there.

# *Madcap*

"An amazing improvement in memory,"
about a brain-zapping cap*
(so says one news correspondent),
with electrodes that do attract.
So you test 20 minutes on each of four days,
but do you take a nap?
And what are the real results to be had?
Is it really now time to clap?

You can remember four to six more words
than before the electrical insult,
but it lasts only about a month;
will cost justify the result?
Touted by some as a miracle,
no word on how long to market,
no word on how drug companies will profit;
a bonanza, I will bet.

"Quite remarkable" says a neurologist,
but no long-term results are defined.
Meantime Alzheimer's marches on
with women on the front lines.**
Just what I need, when I expect to live
another five to twenty years?
So with a month's improvement in memory,
will I really be so pleased?

--------

*https://www.nbcnews.com/health/health-news/brain-zapping-cap-appears-boost-memory-least-1-month-early-research-fi-rcna43949 (August 22, 2022)
**Significantly (about 65%) more women than men suffer from Alzheimers. Could that have something to do with insufficient research funding?

I can tell you about something truly miraculous
if you can find just 88 keys–
piano lessons fire all parts of the brain
and more neuron connections beget.*
I'll take my *Duchess* in all her finery
compared to the alien cap.
I'll be diligent now to practice and learn–
this new "miracle" is purely madcap.

————

**Daniel J. Levitin, *This is Your Brain on Music: The Science
of a Human Obsession*. Dr. Levitin is a neuroscientist, musician,
author, and James McGill Professor Emeritus of Psychology,
McGill University.

## Grace

She had a happy life, but never was a wife
nor mom to boot: that did not suit
the life she sought to live with little strife.

She never did sit back, enjoy the slack,
not fend off attack by misogynist men,
or give in to sexist sins of so many in her path.

She laughed a lot, listened to her mom,
then tossed out what was wrong
for her, not mom.

With errors made she suffered, yes,
but in the end, reason won
and humor, too—

The salve for life's wounds;
and she changed,
and grew.

We must all courtesans be,
brave witches and warlocks, too,
ignore those Puritans who seek to claim
all virtue, but pleasure they do eschew.

We must all bliss pursue,
and war against those who would
rain on our parade,
and gleefully degrade
our hedonistic bent sublime.

We must all liberties embrace,
as those brave souls do
who by others will be
misunderstood at the least,
rejected at worst, and said to be cursed
when we associate with those
who choose bliss, but others readily dismiss.

We must take care to reject
folks like poor Hanslick* who was seriously bent,
his time misspent in defending as rot
the body divine, the senses sublime
while making music or love
that he found poppycock.

We must avoid chains they seek to apply
to us free spirits who dance in the glee
and float on the wind of sensuous sounds,
choose pleasure as we must, in trust
that the day and this life will soon pass away
if we waste time in denying
the pleasure principle–those apt words
for coming "to our senses" is our ultimate reward.

---

*Eduard Hanslick (1854-1885), *The Beautiful in Music*, regarded
physiological or psychological responses as "pathological."

# A Song: Our Happy Place

When nature calls
I can't forestall
the siren call,
but walk with grace
in that cool, green place.

It's on a peaceful beach
in a state of bliss,
I hear the ocean
kiss the sand
as waves reach the land.

CHORUS: There are places in the world
that we inhabit
that feel so fine,
where we unwind
in our happy place.

With gentle touch and word,
so many times
you gift respite
and more there
in what we share,

Or a memory of mom,
her perfumed lotion
envelops me
as she softly
kisses me good night.

CHORUS: There are places in the world
that we inhabit
that feel so fine,
where we unwind
in our happy place.

# Magician

Magician not in word or deed
but a simple woman
who's lived a life complex, it's true!
Her visage does belie
the many dreams that were hers
through effort long and hard,
until at last her hair went down
and up the rope she climbed
to reach for stars, and whirling 'round
to dream some more in hope.

Then floating there, at last to show
her soul in all bespoke
splendor, as is given then
to each of us in turn
to shine our light to all the world
and share lessons that we've learned.

♪♫♪